Bundt Cake Recipes For Any Special Occasion

Coen .U Stone

All rights reserved. Copyright © 2024 Coen .U Stone

COPYRIGHT © 2024 Coen .U Stone

All rights reserved.

No part of this book must be reproduced, stored in a retrieval system, or shared by any means, electronic, mechanical, photocopying, recording, or otherwise, without written permission from the publisher.

Every precaution has been taken in the preparation of this book; still the publisher and author assume no responsibility for errors or omissions. Nor do they assume any liability for damages resulting from the use of the information contained herein.

Legal Notice:

This book is copyright protected and is only meant for your individual use. You are not allowed to amend, distribute, sell, use, quote or paraphrase any of its part without the written consent of the author or publisher.

Introduction

Embark on a flavorful journey through the world of bundt cakes with this book. Each page of this cookbook unveils an array of mouthwatering creations that promise to elevate your baking endeavors to new heights.

Indulge in the timeless allure of the "White Bundt," where simplicity meets elegance in every moist crumb. Or succumb to the decadent charm of the "Chocolate Bundt," a rich and velvety delight that satisfies even the most discerning chocolate lover.

Experience the warmth of home with the comforting "Apples and Cinnamon Bundt," where the aroma of spice-infused apples fills the air with irresistible allure. For a burst of citrusy delight, the "Lime and Coconut Bundt" beckons with its tropical essence, transporting you to sun-drenched shores with each bite.

Dive into the playful world of whimsical bundt cakes with creations like the "Hedgehog Bundt" or the captivating swirls of the "Marble Bundt," where artistry and flavor collide in delightful harmony. Savor the tangy sweetness of the "Cheese and Cranberries Bundt" or the nutty richness of the "Nutella Bundt," each offering a unique culinary adventure.

From classics like the "Simple Bundt" to innovative gems like the "Fantasy Bundt," this cookbook offers something for every palate and occasion. Whether you're craving the comforting embrace of tradition or the thrill of culinary experimentation, this book is your passport to bundt cake bliss.

With its irresistible array of flavors, textures, and aromas, this cookbook is destined to become a cherished companion in your baking repertoire. So gather your ingredients, preheat your oven, and let the magic of bundt cakes unfold with each delectable recipe.

Contents

- (1) White Bundt 1
- (2) Chocolate Bundt 3
- (3) Apples and Cinnamon Bundt 5
- (4) Triple Nickel Bundt 7
- (5) Hedgehog Bundt 9
- (6) Marble Bundt 12
- (7) Cheese and Cranberries Bundt 14
- (8) Sour Cherries Bundt 16
- (9) Lime and Coconut Bundt 18
- (10) Simple Bundt 21
- (11) Dark Bundt 23
- (12) Student's Bundt 25
- (13) Fantasy Bundt 28
- (14) Fragrant Bundt 30
- (15) Refreshing Bundt 32
- (16) Rum Bundt 34
- (17) Sweet Secret Bundt 36
- (18) Gala Bundt 38
- (19) Seventh Heaven Bundt 40
- (20) Nutella Bundt 42
- (21) Drunken Bundt Cake 44
- (22) Moonlight Bundt 46
- (23) Coffee Bundt 48
- (24) Raisa Bundt 50
- (25) Love Secret Bundt 53
- (26) Jaffa bundt 55
- (27) Mini Plum Bundt Cakes 58
- (28) Vanilla and Strawberries Bundt 60
- (29) Snow Peaks Bundt 63
- (30) Granny's Chocolate Bundt 65

- (31) Glazed Bundt Cake 67
- (32) Vermouth Bundt..69
- (33) Mini Bundt Cakes with Cream 71
- (34) Colorful Bundt...74
- (35) Chocolate Bundt...76

(1) White Bundt

You'll find that this cake is fragrant, moist, and elegant. If you are serving it for kids sprinkle with candy crumbs or sprinkles. For some other occasions, use the bundt as a flower vase and place some marzipan or gum paste flowers in it. Serve with tea or white wine.

Makes: 16

Preparation Time: 10 minutes

Total Cook Time: 40 minutes

List of Ingredients:

For batter:

- Greek yogurt, 1 cup
- Vegetable oil, ¾ cup
- Eggs, 2
- Lemon zest, 1 teaspoon
- Lemon juice, 2 teaspoons

- Sugar, 13 ½ oz.
- Plain flour, 10 ½ oz. and some for dusting
- Baking powder, 1 packet

For glaze:

- Confectioners' sugar, 4 ⅓ oz.
- Lemon juice, 2 teaspoons

MMMMMMMMMMMMMMMMMMMMMMMMMMMMMMM

Methods:

For batter:

1. In a mixing bowl, combine the eggs and sugar. Beat with a hand mixer until pale and foamy.

2. Add all of the other ingredients. Stir well to create a smooth batter.

3. Pour the batter into a greased and floured bundt pan and bake in a preheated oven at 350 °F for 40 minutes.

For glaze:

1. In a bowl, combine the sugar and lemon juice and whisk until smooth.

2. Drizzle over a lukewarm bundt and leave to harden.

(2) Chocolate Bundt

Happiness is found in the small things. Chocolate cake, pleasant company (which will be drawn to your kitchen when you're baking this bundt), soft music, and a glass of sweet red wine are all some of those small things.

Makes: 24

Preparation Time: 15 minutes

Total Cook Time: 40 minutes

List of Ingredients:

- Baking chocolate, ¼ lbs.

- Raisins, ⅓ cup
- Butter, ¾ cups
- Plain flour, 1 ⅔ cups
- Eggs, 3
- Baking powder, 1 packet
- Milk, ⅖ cup
- Coffee, 1 tablespoon
- Confectioners sugar, 3 ⅕ oz.

MMMMMMMMMMMMMMMMMMMMMMMMMMMMMM

Methods:

1. Melt the butter in a saucepan over low heat. Add the chocolate which has been broken into pieces. Gently stir until it mixes well.

2. Remove from heat and mix in the milk and coffee.

3. Add the eggs. Mix everything well with a hand mixer.

4. Fold in the flour, baking powder, raisins, and confectioners sugar.

5. Pour the dough into a greased twelve cavity mini bundt pan. The mixture yields two batches. Bake for 20 minutes in a preheated oven at 400 °F.

(3) Apples and Cinnamon Bundt

Here is another recipe that combines apples and cinnamon. It's simple to make and full of extraordinary flavor. Because this cookbook is looking after people that haven't made bundt cakes, this recipe is perfect for those that are starting out. It's great for breakfast with tea, coffee, or milk.

Makes: 16

Preparation Time: 20

Total Cook Time: 45 minutes

List of Ingredients:

- Apple, 1, large
- Eggs, 3
- Sugar, 5 ¼ oz.
- Half & half, ⅘ cup
- Vegetable oil, ⅖ cup
- Plain flour, 7 ½ oz.
- Baking powder, 1 packet
- Raisins, 2 oz.
- Cinnamon, 1 teaspoon
- Rum, 1 shot
- Butter, for greasing.

MMMMMMMMMMMMMMMMMMMMMMMMMMMMMMMMM

Methods:

1. Sprinkle raisins with rum. Set them aside while they soak.

2. Core the apple and cut it into cubes that are roughly a quarter of an inch in size.

3. In a bowl, sift together the flour and baking powder. Set aside.

4. In a mixing bowl, combine the sugar and eggs. Beat with a hand mixer until pale and foamy.

5. Continue to mix. Add the vegetable oil and half & half. Mix until everything is combined well.

6. Add the flour. Stir well to combine.

7. Pat the raisins dry with a paper towel and add them to the batter. Stir to mix.

8. Grease a bundt pan with butter and pour the batter in. Bake in a preheated oven at 350 °F for 45 minutes.

(4) Triple Nickel Bundt

How can you remember this recipe easily? This bundt cake has ratios of ingredients which are easy to remember as 3-2-1: 3 (5 eggs, 5 tablespoons of flour, 5 tablespoons of sugar), 2 (tablespoons of oil or butter), 1 (packet of baking powder). It will amaze you with its soft, velvety texture and flavor. This may be easy to make, but it doesn't last long. Serve with coffee or white wine.

Makes: 16

Preparation Time: 20 minutes

Total Cook Time: 45 minutes

List of Ingredients:

- Egg whites, 5

- Plain flour, 5 Tablespoons
- Sugar, 5 Tablespoons
- Sunflower oil or melted butter, 2 Tablespoons
- Baking powder, 1 packet
- Raisins, ½ cup
- Almonds, ½ cup, roughly chopped
- Walnuts, ½ cup, roughly chopped
- Butter, a knob, for greasing

MMMMMMMMMMMMMMMMMMMMMMMMMMMMMMMM

Methods:

1. Put the egg whites and sugar in a mixing bowl. Whisk until stiff peaks form.

2. Add the sunflower oil or melted butter. Be careful if you are using butter. It will need to be cooled to room temperature. Mix for some 5-10 seconds.

3. Fold in the egg whites, flour, and baking powder. Stir gently but long enough for the flour to mix well with egg whites.

4. Fold into the mixture the other List of Ingredients: raisins, almonds, and walnuts.

5. Pour the mixture into the greased bundt pan and bake in a preheated oven at 350 °F for 45-50 minutes.

(5) Hedgehog Bundt

The bundt has a very characteristic and intoxicating flavor from the combination of almonds and poppy seeds. You can be playful when decorating it and stick almond sticks or halved almond slices to make it look like a hedgehog. Kids will love it. Serve this cake with tea, milk, coffee, or red wine.

Makes:

Preparation Time: 55-60

Total Cook Time: 1 hour

List of Ingredients:

For batter:

- Butter, 6 ⅓ oz.
- Sugar, 6 ⅓ oz.
- Ground poppy seeds, 6 ⅓ oz.
- Ground almonds, 6 ⅓ oz.
- Eggs, 6

For chocolate glaze:

- Chocolate, 4 ⅕ oz.
- Butter, 3 ½ oz.

Optionally:

- Almond sticks or slices, ½ cup

MMMMMMMMMMMMMMMMMMMMMMMMMMMMMMMM

Methods:

1. In a mixing bowl, combine the butter and sugar. Beat the mixture with a hand mixer until pale white in color and all of the sugar is dissolved.

2. Add one egg yolk at the time. Mix with a hand mixer each time to incorporate.

3. Add the almonds and poppy seeds. Stir to combine.

4. In a separate mixing bowl, beat the egg whites until a stiff peaks form.

5. Transfer the egg whites into the yolk mixture and stir gently to combine well.

6. Pour the batter into a greased bundt pan and bake in a preheated oven at 320 °F for an hour.

7. Once baked, transfer the cake to a serving platter. Let it cool for 30 minutes.

8. When the bundt is cool, melt chocolate and butter in a saucepan over low heat while gently stirring. Drizzle this chocolate glaze over the bundt.

(6)   Marble Bundt

This bundt is simple to prepare, and the cuts look just like a real marble. Kids will love it. It's a great snack with milk, but it also goes well with coffee or tea.

Makes: 16

Preparation Time: 25 minutes

Total Cook Time: 50 minutes

List of Ingredients:

- Eggs, 5
- Sugar, 10 Tablespoons
- Sunflower or rapeseed oil, 10 Tablespoons

- Plain flour, 10 Tablespoons and bit more for dusting
- Cocoa powder, 2 Tablespoons
- Vanilla sugar, 1 packet

MMMMMMMMMMMMMMMMMMMMMMMMMMMMMMMM

Methods:

1. Crack the eggs in a mixing bowl with sugar. Mix with a hand mixer until the mixture becomes foamy.

2. Add the oil and mix with mixer until well combined.

3. Divide the mixture in half. In one half, mix in cocoa powder. In the other, mix in vanilla sugar. One packet of store-bought vanilla sugar can be substituted with one teaspoon of vanilla extract or two teaspoons of homemade vanilla sugar.

4. Dust the bundt pan with flour. Then pour in alternatively the cocoa and vanilla mixtures with a tablespoon.

5. Bake in a preheated oven at 350 °F for 50 minutes.

(7) Cheese and Cranberries Bundt

This is one of the moistest and softest bundts. Cranberries and cheese give it a nice flavor. You will not err if you want to substitute cranberries with raisins, but this way it's a great fall treat. Serve with soft drinks or white wine.

Makes: 16

Preparation Time: 10-15 minutes

Total Cook Time: 1 hour

List of Ingredients:

- Butter, 6 ½ oz.
- Cream cheese, 7 oz.
- Lemon zest
- Sugar, 9 ½ oz.
- Plain flour, 13 oz.
- Baking powder, 1 packet
- Dried cranberries, 1 cup
- Eggs, 3

Methods:

1. Place the butter and cream cheese in a mixing bowl. Use a hand mixer set on a low speed to soften and start combining the ingredients.

2. Add the sugar to the mixing bowl and increase the speed of the mixer. Mix until all of the sugar dissolves and the mixture is pale and velvety.

3. Add one egg at a time while mixing. Make sure to mix more after adding each one to incorporate it well.

4. Sift the flour and baking powder into the mix. Stir to combine.

5. Add the cranberries and stir gently to combine.

6. Pour the batter in to a greased bundt pan and then bake in the preheated oven at 350 °F for 1 hour.

7. Transfer to a serving platter and ice with an icing sugar or icing of your liking.

(8)   Sour Cherries Bundt

This is a very versatile bundt batter. Instead of sour cherries, you can use almost any other fruit like grated apples, cherries, raspberries, or strawberries. It goes well as dessert along with digestif or coffee.

Makes: 16

Preparation Time: 25 minutes

Total Cook Time: 40 minutes

List of Ingredients:

- Eggs, 4, separated whites and yolks
- Sugar, 1 ½ cup
- Boiling water, 10 Tablespoons

- Sunflower or rapeseed oil, 5 Tablespoons
- Plain flour, 2 cups
- Baking powder, 1 packet
- Pitted tart cherries, 2 cups, well drained

MMMMMMMMMMMMMMMMMMMMMMMMMMMMMMMMM

Methods:

1. Place the egg yolks and sugar in a mixing bowl. Mix using a hand mixer until the sugar melts.

2. Add boiling water and continue mixing until the mixture becomes almost white.

3. In another mixing bowl, mix the egg whites until they form stiff peaks.

4. Combine the egg yolks and egg whites. Stir well but gently.

5. In this mixture, add the flour and baking powder. Mix well but gently.

6. Pour the mixture into the greased bundt pan and strew tart cherries over the mixture.

7. Bake in a preheated oven at 400 °F for 40 minutes.

(9)   Lime and Coconut Bundt

When I made this bundt for the first time, I was a bit skeptical about the lime and coconut flavor combination. I was definitely wrong. The gorgeous, refreshing flavor I was rewarded with has made this bundt one of my favorites. A bit of effort is definitely worthwhile in this case. This cake goes well with green tea or coffee.

Makes: 16

Preparation Time: 65 minutes

Total Cook Time: 45 minutes

List of Ingredients:

For batter:

- Plain flour, 9 oz.
- Baking powder, 2 teaspoons
- Sugar, 6 oz.
- Lime zest
- Eggs, 3, whisked
- Butter, 5 ¼ oz., melted and cooled
- Half & half, 10 Tablespoons
- Coconut flour, 3 ⅕ oz.

For syrup:

- Lime juice, ⅖ cup
- Sugar, 6 oz.
- Water, 3 Tablespoons

MMMMMMMMMMMMMMMMMMMMMMMMMMMMMMM

Methods:

1. Sift the flour and the baking powder into a bowl.

2. Add all of the other ingredients, except for the coconut flour, and whisk everything together.

3. Add the coconut flour and stir to combine.

4. Pour the batter into a greased bundt pan and bake in a preheated oven at 350 °F for 45 minutes.

5. When the bundt is baked, leave it in the pan while making syrup.

6. Place all of the ingredients in a saucepan. Bring the mixture to a boil while gently stirring. Leave the mixture to boil for 2 minutes without stirring and then pour over the bundt.

7. Leave the bundt to completely cool for 45 minutes and then transfer to a serving platter.

(10) Simple Bundt

If you ever wished to make a bundt in just 10 minutes, then this is the recipe for you. You can serve it as a dessert with a tablespoon of jello or ice cream, or just dusted with confectioners sugar. Simple, lite, and flavorful.

Makes: 16

Preparation Time: 10 minutes

Total Cook Time: 30 minutes

List of Ingredients:

- Eggs, 4
- Sugar, 1 cup
- Half and half, 1 cup
- Plain flour, 2 cups
- Baking powder, 1 packet
- Vanilla sugar, 1 packet, can be substituted with 1 teaspoon vanilla extract or 2 teaspoons homemade

vanilla sugar
- Sunflower or rapeseed oil, ½ cup

Methods:

1. In a mixing bowl, mix eggs and sugar until foamy and light yellow in color.

2. Mix in the rest of ingredients and stir well to combine.

3. Pour the mixture into the greased bundt pan and bake in preheated oven at 400 °F for 30 minutes.

(11) Dark Bundt

You will be hard-pressed to find a simpler recipe for a bundt that has a better chocolate flavor. If you serve it in the morning, serve it with milk, coffee, or tea. As a dessert, serve it with red wine or coffee.

Makes: 16

Preparation Time: 5-7 minutes

Total Cook Time: 40 minutes

List of Ingredients:

For batter:

- Sugar, ⅘ cup
- Plain flour, 1 ⅗ cup and some for dusting
- Butter, 4 oz., melted and cooled to room temperature
- Raisins, 2 oz.
- Chopped walnuts, 4 oz.
- Half & half, ⅘ cup
- Baking powder, 1 packet
- Cocoa powder, 1 tablespoon
- Apricot jam, 3 Tablespoons

For chocolate glaze:

- Baking chocolate, 4 oz.
- Butter, 2 oz.
- Rum, 1 shot, or few drops of flavoring

MMMMMMMMMMMMMMMMMMMMMMMMMMMMMMMM

Methods:

For batter:

1. Place the sugar and half & half in a mixing bowl. Whisk until all of the sugar dissolves.

2. Add all of the other ingredients and whisk until everything is mixed well.

3. Pour the batter into a greased and floured bundt pan. Bake in an oven preheated to 480 °F. Immediately lower the temperature to 400 °F and bake for 40 minutes.

For chocolate glaze:

1. Place all of the ingredients into a saucepan and melt over low heat while gently stirring.

2. Place the still warm bunt on a serving platter and pour warm glaze over it.

(12) Student's Bundt

Now you are wondering why this is a "student's" bundt. It is named because it has the taste and smell of home and family. Everything students miss while they are at their campus. Treat your student with this bundt cake. Surprise them and their roommates. This bundt keeps well for several days and is gluten-free.

Makes: 16

Preparation Time: 25 minutes

Total Cook Time: 45 minutes

List of Ingredients:

For batter:

- Egg yolks, 9
- Lemon zest, of one lemon
- Confectioners sugar 1 ¼ cup
- Ground walnuts, 9 oz.
- Raisins, 4 ½ oz.

For Italian meringue:

- Egg whites, 4
- Sugar, 1 cup
- Water, less than a cup
- Lemon juice or cream of tartar, ½ teaspoons
- Cooking thermometer

MMMMMMMMMMMMMMMMMMMMMMMMMMMMMMM

Methods:

For batter:

1. Place the egg yolks and confectioners sugar in a mixing bowl. Mix with a hand mixer until foamy.

2. Add the lemon zest, walnuts, and raisins. Stir well to combine.

3. Pour the mixture into a greased bundt pan and bake in a preheated oven at 275 °F for 45 minutes.

4. Once baked, transfer the bundt to a serving platter. Leave it to rest overnight.

5. The next day, frost with the Italian meringue.

For Italian meringue:

1. In a mixing bowl, combine the eggs and lemon juice or cream of tartar. Mix with a hand mixer on low speed until it starts to foam.

2. In a saucepan, combine the sugar and enough water to cover it. Place the mixture over high heat, stir until it starts boiling. When it

boils, place a cooking thermometer in and let the mixture continue to boil until it reaches 240-245 °F.

3. While the sugar is boiling, continue mixing the egg whites with a hand mixer on medium speed until soft peaks form.

4. Remove the sugar from heat and start pouring in a thin stream into the egg whites while mixing them with a hand mixer on medium speed.

5. When all of the syrup is poured increase the speed of mixer and mix until stiff peaks form.

Optionally, sprinkle raisins over the Italian meringue or scorch the surface using a torch.

(13) Fantasy Bundt

Can you say anything about the combination of walnuts and chocolate beside yum? This cake is excellent as a snack or dessert after dinner with coffee or red wine.

Makes: 16

Preparation Time: 25 minutes

Total Cook Time: 50 minutes

List of Ingredients:

- Butter, ⅔ cup
- Sugar, ¾ cup
- Eggs, 5, separated whites and yolks
- Baking chocolate, 2 oz., grated or chopped

- Raisins, 2 oz.
- Walnuts, 2 oz., chopped
- Plain flour, 1 ½ cup
- Ground clove or cinnamon, a pinch

Methods:

1. In a mixing bowl, combine the butter and sugar. Mix using a hand mixer until foamy.

2. Add the mixture to the egg yolks and mix well.

3. In a separate mixing bowl, beat the egg whites until they form stiff peaks.

4. Add the egg whites to the butter mixture. Stir well to combine.

5. Add the chocolate, raisins, walnuts, flour, and clove or cinnamon. Stir everything well.

6. Pour the mixture into a greased bundt pan and bake in preheated oven at 320 °F for 50 minutes.

(14) Fragrant Bundt

This bundt will tickle all of your senses. It takes a little bit of time for the fragrances of vanilla, raisins, and walnuts to spread through your kitchen. If you wish so you can substitute walnuts with hazelnuts or almonds. Liberally dust this cake with icing sugar and serve it with white wine or soft drinks.

Makes: 16

Preparation Time: 20 minutes

Total Cook Time: 50 minutes

List of Ingredients:

- Butter, 9 oz.
- Sugar, 9 oz.
- Eggs, 5, separated whites and yolks
- Milk, ⅖ cup
- Lemon zest, of half lemon
- Vanilla sugar, 1 packet
- Plain flour, 16 oz.
- Baking powder, 1 packet
- Raisins, 3 ½ oz.
- Chopped walnuts, 2 oz.
- Confectioners sugar, ½ cup
- Vanilla powder, 1 teaspoon

MMMMMMMMMMMMMMMMMMMMMMMMMMMMMMMM

Methods:

1. Sift the confectioners sugar and vanilla powder in a bowl and set aside.

2. In a mixing bowl, combine the butter, egg yolks, and sugar. Beat with a hand mixer until all of the sugar dissolves.

3. Add the milk, rum, lemon zest, vanilla sugar, half of the flour, and baking powder. Stir well.

4. In another mixing bowl, beat the egg whites with a hand mixer until a stiff peaks form.

5. Add the rest of flour and beaten egg whites to the egg yolk mixture. Gently stir to combine.

6. Pour in the batter to a greased bundt pan and bake in a preheated oven at 400 °F for 50 minutes.

7. When done, transfer the cake to a serving platter to cool for 15 minutes. Then dust with confectioners sugar.

(15)   Refreshing Bundt

Mix of raisins and lemon zest gives a refreshing note to this seemingly plain bundt with yeast. Excellent as breakfast with milk, tea or coffee.

Makes: 16

Preparation Time: 1 hour 15 minutes

Total Cook Time: 40 minutes

List of Ingredients:

- Warm milk, 1 cup
- Butter, 1 cup
- Egg yolks, 8
- Strong flour, 2 cups

- Confectioners sugar, 1 cup
- Dry yeast, 1 teaspoon
- Lemon zest, of 1 lemon
- Raisins, 2 oz.

MMMMMMMMMMMMMMMMMMMMMMMMMMMMMMMMMM

Methods:

1. Mix the dry yeast with warm milk. Set aside.

2. In a mixing bowl, combine the butter and sugar. Use a hand mixer to mix until foamy.

3. Add to this mixture to egg yolks and lemon zest. Mix well.

4. Add the milk with yeast. Stir well to combine.

5. Add the flour and raisins. Beat with a mixing spoon for about 30 minutes.

6. Pour in a bundt pan and leave it in a warm place to rise almost to the brim of the pan.

7. Bake in a preheated oven at 350 °F for 40 minutes.

(16) Rum Bundt

This cake is soft, moist, and has a refreshing flavor. It's very easy to make, but the royal glaze icing makes it look amazing on a serving platter. Serve with a beverage of your choice.

Makes: 16

Preparation Time: 35 minutes

Total Cook Time: 45 minutes

List of Ingredients:

- Plain flour, 16 ounces and some for flouring

- Sugar, 5 ¼ oz. and 1 ¾ oz.
- Eggs, 3 whole and an egg white
- Vanilla sugar, 1 packet
- Baking powder, 1 packet
- Water, 6 Tablespoons
- Dark rum, 6 Tablespoons
- Confectioners sugar, 7 oz.
- Lemon juice, 2 Tablespoons

MMMMMMMMMMMMMMMMMMMMMMMMMMMMMMM

Methods:

1. In a bowl, sift the flour and baking powder. Set aside.

2. In a mixing bowl, combine a quarter ounce of sugar, eggs, and vanilla sugar. Beat with a hand mixer until pale and foamy.

3. Lower the mixing speed to low and start adding flour to the mixture a tablespoon at a time.

4. Grease and flour a bundt pan and pour the mixture in. Bake in a preheated oven at 350 °F for 45 minutes.

5. When the bundt is baked, combine the rum, water, and one and three quarters of an ounce of sugar in a saucepan. Bring to a boil and let it cook for a minute until all of the alcohol evaporates. Pour this syrup over the bundt while it is still in the pan and let it soak while making the royal icing.

6. In a bowl, combine the egg whites and whisk a bit. Start adding sugar one tablespoon at the time and whisk until smooth. Now put the icing on the cake.

(17)   Sweet Secret Bundt

It's a well-known fact that apples and cinnamon go hand in hand. But if you add cognac or whiskey, it's an even better combination. This bundt is a great dessert served along with the same spirit you added. This can be served to children as the alcohol evaporates during baking.

Makes: 16

Preparation Time: 20 minutes

Total Cook Time: 35 minutes

List of Ingredients:

- Apples, 4-5, medium size, cored and sliced to half inch

- Butter, ½ cup
- Sugar, 2 cups
- Walnuts, 2 oz., chopped
- Cinnamon, 1 teaspoon
- Plain flour, 1 ½ cup
- Eggs, 4
- Baking powder, 1 packet
- Cognac, whiskey, or some other spirit, 1 shot

MMMMMMMMMMMMMMMMMMMMMMMMMMMMMMMM

Methods:

1. Melt the butter and pour it into a bundt pan.

2. Pour one cup of sugar into the butter and place apple slices over it.

3. In a mixing bowl, beat the eggs with a cup of sugar until foamy and light yellow in color.

4. Add the flour, baking powder, and spirit to the egg mixture. Mix well to combine.

5. Pour this mixture over the apple slices.

6. Bake in a preheated oven at 400 °F for 35 minutes.

(18) Gala Bundt

This is an old-school, festive bundt. We bring you this recipe in hope of returning the old glory of a simple but also a bit haute cuisine chocolate bundt. Kids will love it with milk, and you can enjoy it with a glass of good red wine or French press coffee.

Makes:

Preparation Time: 20 minutes

Total Cook Time: 45 minutes

List of Ingredients:

- Flour, 10 ½ oz.
- Baking powder, 1 packet
- Confectioners sugar, 5 ¼ oz.
- Butter, 5 ¼ oz., melted

- Baking chocolate, 2 ½ oz., chopped
- Eggs, 4
- Milk, 5 Tablespoons

MMMMMMMMMMMMMMMMMMMMMMMMMMMMMMMMM

Methods:

1. In a mixing bowl, combine the sugar and butter. Beat with a hand mixer until the sugar dissolves.

2. Add the eggs and milk. Stir well to combine.

3. Sift a third of the flour into the mixing bowl and stir to combine. Sift another third with the baking powder. Mix well. Add the rest of flour and chocolate, then mix again.

4. Pour the batter into a greased bundt pan and bake in a preheated oven at 350 °F for 45 minutes.

5. Leave the bundt to cool in the pan for 30 minutes. Transfer the cake to a serving platter and sprinkle with the icing sugar if you want.

(19) Seventh Heaven Bundt

A strange name for any cake, isn't it? This bundt has to be baked a day ahead. It's much more flavorful when all ingredients have time to release their aromas and give a unique taste to this bundt cake. The chocolate glaze is a bit elastic thus it cuts easily without cracking. It is excellent as a dessert with a coffee or red wine.

Makes: 16

Preparation Time: 20 minutes

Total Cook Time: 40 minutes

List of Ingredients:

For batter:

- Butter, ⅝ cup
- Confectioners sugar, 18 Tablespoons
- Eggs, 4, separated yolks and whites

- Baking chocolate, 1 ½ oz.
- Almonds, 3 ½ oz., grated
- Plain flour, ½ cup

For glaze:

- Baking chocolate, ¾ oz.
- Milk, ⅕ cup
- Sugar cubes, 6

MMMMMMMMMMMMMMMMMMMMMMMMMMMMMMM

Methods:

For batter:

1. In a saucepan, mix the butter, sugar, and egg yolks. Over medium-low heat, whisk until it becomes foamy.

2. Remove from heat and add the chocolate and almonds. Stir gently until chocolate melts.

3. In a mixing bowl, beat the egg whites with a mixer until stiff peaks.

4. Transfer the beaten egg whites into the saucepan with egg yolk mixture. Add flour and slowly stir everything to combine.

5. Pour the mixture into a greased bundt pan and bake for 40 minutes in a preheated oven at 350 °F.

6. Transfer the cake onto a serving platter. When cool, pour the glaze over.

For glaze:

1. In a bain-marie or a saucepan place the baking chocolate, milk, and sugar cubes. Whisk over steam until everything melts.

2. While glaze is still warm, pour over the bundt cake and let it set.

(20) Nutella Bundt

Who could resist a Nutella bundt? This nectar of gods goes into the batter and is used as the glaze as well. This is an excellent bundt that will satisfy any Nutella junky. But it will also be delicious when they feel like sharing.

Makes: 16

Preparation Time: 50 minutes

Total Cook Time: 45 minutes

List of Ingredients:

- Plain flour, 2 cups
- Baking powder, 1 packet
- Eggs, 4
- Vegetable oil, 4/5 cup
- Vanilla sugar, 1 teaspoon

- Sugar, 1 ⅗ cup, divided in half
- Milk, ⅘ cup
- Nutella, 2 13 oz. jars
- Water, ⅘ cup

MMMMMMMMMMMMMMMMMMMMMMMMMMMMMMMM

Methods:

1. Sift the flour and baking powder into a bowl and set aside.

2. In a mixing bowl, combine the eggs, vanilla sugar, and half of the sugar. Beat with a hand mixer until pale in color and foamy.

3. While continuing to mix, add the oil and milk. Beat until combined.

4. Add one jar of Nutella and stir to combine.

5. Now add the sifted flour and baking powder. Gently stir to make some smooth batter.

6. Pour the batter into a greased bundt pan and bake in preheated oven at 350 °F for 45 minutes.

7. While the bundt is baking, place the other half of the sugar and water in a saucepan. Bring the mixture to a boil while stirring constantly. When it starts boiling, stop stirring and let it boil for 2 minutes.

8. The content of the second Nutella jar should be transferred to a microwave-safe container and microwave for 1 minute. After taking it out, whisk it until it reaches an even consistency.

9. When the bundt is baked pour the sugar syrup over it and leave the cake in the pan to cool for 30 minutes.

10. Transfer to a serving platter and glaze with the softened Nutella.

(21) Drunken Bundt Cake

Even before you finish reading this recipe you will know what to expect. There's alcohol involved. In all honesty, it's a small amount which evaporates during baking. Kids will still be able to eat it. If you decide to serve it as a dessert, serve the cake with coffee or red wine.

Makes: 16

Preparation Time: 25 minutes

Total Cook Time: 50 minutes

List of Ingredients:

- Butter, 2 ½ oz.
- Sugar, ¾ cup
- Eggs, 6, separated yolks and whites
- Baking chocolate, 3 ⅕ oz.

- Plain flour, ⅓ cup
- Baking powder, 1 ½ teaspoons
- Breadcrumbs, 2 Tablespoons, fine dry
- Rum, 1 shot
- Ground walnuts, 1 ½ cup
- Whipping cream, ⅘ cup

MMMMMMMMMMMMMMMMMMMMMMMMMMMMMMMM

Methods:

1. Melt the chocolate in a saucepan over low heat. Set aside to cool for a bit.

2. While the chocolate is cooling, mix the egg yolks, butter, and sugar in another bowl. Mix with a mixer until foamy.

3. Slowly drizzle the chocolate in the mixing bowl with egg yolk mixture while mixing with mixer.

4. Sift the flour and baking powder into the mixing bowl. Stir well to combine.

5. In another mixing bowl, beat the egg whites until they form stiff peaks.

6. Pour the egg whites, ground walnuts, and breadcrumbs soaked in rum into egg yolks mixture. Gently stir everything to combine.

7. Pour the mixture into a greased bundt pan and bake in preheated oven at 350 °F for 45-50 minutes.

8. Transfer to a serving platter and drizzle with chocolate glaze.

(22) Moonlight Bundt

"You could hold moonlight in your hands." - "Moonlight" Ariana Grande

And you really can, if you make this bundt. Serve this cake with tea, coffee, or white wine. Then you'll be able to hold the moonlight.

Makes: 16

Preparation Time: 25 minutes

Total Cook Time: 55 minutes

List of Ingredients:

- Eggs, 3, yolks and whites separated
- Plain flour, 9 Tablespoons
- Sugar, 9 Tablespoons
- Vegetable oil, 9 Tablespoons

- Milk, 9 Tablespoons
- Baking powder, 1 teaspoon
- Vanilla sugar, 2 packets
- Lemon zest, of one lemon
- Chopped walnuts, 1 oz.
- Sour cherries, 5 oz.
- Butter, 1 oz., melted and cooled to room temperature
- Breadcrumbs, ½ cup

MMMMMMMMMMMMMMMMMMMMMMMMMMMMMMMMM

Methods:

1. In a mixing bowl, combine the egg yolks and six tablespoons of sugar. Mix with a hand mixer until pale and all of the sugar is dissolved.

2. While continuing to mix, add the vanilla sugar, lemon zest, oil, and milk.

3. In the mixing bowl with the yolk mixture, sift in the flour and baking powder. Mix well.

4. In another mixing bowl, combine the egg whites and three tablespoons of sugar. Beat until stiff peaks form.

5. Fold the egg whites into the egg yolk mixture.

6. Grease the bundt pan with melted butter and coat with breadcrumbs, shaking out the excess.

7. Pour the batter into the pan and then sprinkle chopped walnuts and sour cherries on top.

8. Bake in a preheated oven at 340 °F for 55 minutes.

(23) Coffee Bundt

This bundt cake must be served with coffee or tea. It makes for an excellent breakfast, but it can also be a good dessert too. It's not light, but it goes excellently after a hearty meal. Kids will love it.

Makes: 16

Preparation Time: 20 minutes

Total Cook Time: 45 minutes

List of Ingredients:

- Butter, ⅔ cup
- Egg yolks, 8
- Egg whites, 6

- Sugar, 1 cup
- Ground almonds, 1 ½ cup
- Coffee grounds, 2 teaspoons
- Graham cracker crumbs, 1 tablespoon
- Rum, 1 shot
- Plain flour, 2 Tablespoons
- Apricot jam, ½ cup

MMMMMMMMMMMMMMMMMMMMMMMMMMMMMMMMM

Methods:

1. In a cup or small bowl, put the graham cracker crumbs. Pour rum over them and set aside to soak.

2. In a mixing bowl, place in the egg yolks, sugar, and butter. Mix with a hand mixer until it's paled in color and foamy.

3. Add the ground almonds, coffee grounds, graham cracker crumbs, and flour to the egg yolk mixture. Mix everything well.

4. In another mixing bowl, beat the egg whites until they form stiff peaks.

5. Gently fold in the egg whites to the egg yolk mixture.

6. Pour the mixture into a greased bundt pan. Bake in a preheated oven at 400 °F for 45 minutes.

7. While it bakes, mix the apricot jam with a fork or whisk so it can be spread easily.

8. When the cake is baked, transfer it to a serving platter and glaze with apricot jam.

(24) Raisa Bundt

This bundt is one with an interesting story. Its creation is tied to an apocryphal story. During some formal dinner in honor of the Soviet President Gorbachev, taking place in the Germany, Frau Ilona Getz served this bundt, her creation, as a dessert. President Gorbachev's wife, Raisa, was so impressed by this bundt that she demanded to personally ask Frau Getz for the recipe. Because of this event, Frau Getz named the bundt after Raisa. So, I present you with a recipe for the bundt which entered history books. Serve with white wine, liqueurs, or soft drinks.

Makes: 16

Preparation Time: 1 hour 15 minutes

Total Cook Time: 1 hour

List of Ingredients:

- Butter, 10 ½ oz. and 1 oz. for greasing
- Sugar, 7 oz.
- Vanilla sugar, 1 packet
- Eggs, 5
- Lemon aroma, one vial
- Lemon zest, of half a lemon
- Plain flour, 17 ½ oz.
- Baking powder, 1 packet
- Milk, 6 Tablespoons
- Breadcrumbs, ½ cup
- Icing sugar, ½ cup

MMMMMMMMMMMMMMMMMMMMMMMMMMMMMMMM

Methods:

1. In a bowl, mix together the sugar and vanilla sugar.

2. In a smaller bowl, sift together roughly a quarter of the flour and baking powder.

3. In a mixing bowl, place the butter. Start mixing with a hand mixer set on a low speed. Mix for about 2 minutes, then add a quarter of sugar mix. Mix for another 2 minutes. Continue doing this until all sugar is used. Keep mixing until all of the sugar is dissolved in butter.

4. Add the eggs one at the time while mixing with a hand mixer for about 2 minutes after each egg.

5. Add the lemon aroma and zest while continuing to mix.

6. While continuing to mix on low speed, keep adding two tablespoons of milk followed by a quarter of flour at the time until all milk is used. In the end, mix in the flour previously mixed with baking powder, and mix on low speed until all is combined.

7. Grease a bundt pan with melted butter and coat with breadcrumbs, shaking out the excess.

8. Pour the batter into the bundt pan and bake in a preheated oven at 340 °F for one hour.

9. When baked, leave the cake in the bundt pan to rest for 10 minutes. Then, transfer the cake to a serving platter. Leave it to cool down to room temperature for 30 minutes and then liberally cover with icing sugar.

(25) Love Secret Bundt

Honey, clove, cinnamon, raisins, and more. You've probably stopped wondering why this bundt is named what it is. Serve this particular bundt with white wine. All your senses will enjoy it immensely.

Makes: 16

Preparation Time: 25 minutes

Total Cook Time: 40 minutes

List of Ingredients:

- Butter, 1 cup
- Honey, 1 pint
- Plain flour, 4 cups and some more for dusting
- Eggs, 2
- Egg yolks, 4
- Cinnamon, 1 teaspoon

- Ground clove, ½ teaspoons
- White raisins, 1 cup
- Baking soda, 2 teaspoons
- Chopped walnuts, 2 ½ cups

MMMMMMMMMMMMMMMMMMMMMMMMMMMMMMMM

Methods:

1. Over medium heat, melt the butter and honey in a deep dish.

2. Remove from the heat. Pour in the flour and mix well.

3. Transfer the mixture to a work surface. Knead until the dough is smooth or for about 5-10 minutes. Then, leave the dough to cool covered with a kitchen towel for 10-15 minutes.

4. When it's cooled, mix in all of the other ingredients. Knead for 10 minutes for everything to combine well.

5. Place dough in a well-greased and flour dusted bundt pan. Let it rest for 3 hours in a warm place.

6. Bake in a preheated oven at 350 °F for 40 minutes.

(26) Jaffa bundt

If you want a bundt to have a nice chocolate glaze, then don't pour the glaze onto the bundt while the cake is still hot. The glaze will just slide off. This recipe is a more complex variant of old-school bundt cake recipes. This gorgeous bundt should always be served as a dessert with coffee or red wine.

Makes: 16

Preparation Time: 1 hour

Total Cook Time: 1 hour

List of Ingredients:

- Sugar, 9 oz., divided in half
- Eggs, 5, whites and yolks separated

- Vegetable oil, ⅘ cup
- Plain flour, 10 ⅕ oz.
- Baking powder, 1 packet
- Orange zest, of one large ones
- Freshly squeezed orange juice, of two large oranges, divided in half
- Orange soda, ⅖ cup
- Candied orange peel, 2 oz.
- Baking chocolate, 7 oz., divided in half
- Butter, 1 oz. for greasing and 1 oz. for glaze
- Breadcrumbs, ½ cup

MMMMMMMMMMMMMMMMMMMMMMMMMMMMMMMMM

Methods:

1. In a saucepan, place half of chocolate. Melt it over low heat. Set aside to cool.

2. In a mixing bowl, combine half of sugar and egg yolks. With a hand mixer, beat until pale and foamy.

3. In another mixing bowl, place the other half of the sugar and egg whites. With a hand mixer, beat until hard peaks form.

4. Combine the whites and yolks by gently stirring.

5. While constantly stirring, add one ingredient at the time from the following: oil, orange juice, orange zest, melted chocolate, orange soda, candied orange peel, then the flour and baking powder sifted together.

6. Grease the bundt pan with melted butter and coat with breadcrumbs, shaking out the excess.

7. Pour the batter into the bundt pan and bake in a preheated oven at 340 °F for one hour.

8. When bundt is baked, transfer it to a serving platter. While it's still warm, pour over the rest of orange juice. Let it rest for 30 minutes.

9. While the bundt is resting, prepare the chocolate glaze by melting the other half of the baking chocolate with butter in a saucepan over low heat.

10. When bundt has rested, pour over with chocolate glaze.

(27) Mini Plum Bundt Cakes

These mini bundt cakes are perfect for fruitcake lovers. Kids will love them and ask for more. This works well as breakfast, snack, or dessert. Serve them with coffee, tea, spirits, or white wine.

Makes: 24

Preparation Time: 20 minutes

Total Cook Time: 25 minutes

List of Ingredients:

- Plums, 9 oz., diced to small cubes
- Butter, 1 tablespoon

- Sugar, 4 ½ oz.
- Egg, 1
- Milk, 1 ¼ cup
- Plain flour, 2 cups
- Chopped almonds, 1 ¾ oz.
- Cream cheese, 1 ⅓ cup
- Lemon juice, 2 teaspoons
- Vanilla sugar, 1 packet

MMMMMMMMMMMMMMMMMMMMMMMMMMMMMMMM

Methods:

1. Place the butter and sugar in a mixing bowl. Mix with a hand mixer until foamy.

2. Add an egg and mix well.

3. Slowly pour in milk while mixing until the mixture is smooth.

4. Add the flour, baking powder, almonds, and plums. Mix the ingredients well.

5. Pour the mixture into a greased twelve cavity mini bundt pan. Bake for 25 minutes in a preheated oven at 350 °F.

6. In a mixing bowl, combine the cream cheese, lemon juice, and vanilla sugar. Mix well with a hand mixer. Use this mixture for frosting mini bundt cakes.

(28) Vanilla and Strawberries Bundt

Why does a cake have to be round or square when it can come with a hole in the middle? Serve this bundt with white wine.

Makes: 16

Preparation Time: 35 minutes

Total Cook Time: 90 minutes

List of Ingredients:

For batter:

- Eggs, 4
- Sugar, 7 oz.
- Plain flour, 9 oz.
- Milk, ⅗ cup
- Vegetable oil, ⅗ cup
- Vanilla sugar, 1 packet

- Baking powder, 1 packet
- Baking chocolate, 4 1/5 oz., melted

For filling:

- Milk, 1 pint
- Sugar, 7 Tablespoons
- Instant vanilla pudding mix, 2 packs
- Butter, 3 ½ oz.
- Strawberries, 10 oz., sliced and divided in half

For chocolate glaze:

- Baking chocolate, 3 ½ oz.
- Butter, 2 Tablespoons

MMMMMMMMMMMMMMMMMMMMMMMMMMMMMM

Methods:

For batter:

1. Place the eggs, vanilla sugar, and caster sugar in a mixing bowl. Using a hand mixer, mix until the mixture is foamy and pale.

2. In a separate bowl, sift the flour and baking powder. Add it to yolks mixture and stir well to combine.

3. Add melted chocolate to the mixing bowl. Stir well.

4. Pour the batter into a greased bundt pan and bake in a preheated oven at 400 °F for 15 minutes. Then lower temperature to 300 °F and bake another 30 minutes.

For filling:

1. Place the milk and sugar in a saucepan and bring to a boil.

2. Pour the instant pudding mix in. Stir for two minutes over low heat.

3. Remove from the heat and let it cool to room temperature.

4. While the pudding is cooling, place the butter in a mixing bowl and beat with a hand mixer until foamy and pale in color.

5. When the pudding has cooled, add the butter. Mix them well with a hand mixer on low to medium speed until it is a smooth cream.

For chocolate glaze:

1. Place the butter and chocolate in a saucepan. After the bundt is assembled, melt them over low heat while gently stirring.

Assembly:

1. Cut the bundt horizontally into three even layers.

2. Place the lowest layer on a serving platter and spread half of the filling over it.

3. Spread half of the strawberries on top of filling.

4. Place the middle layer over strawberries and repeat the process of filling. Place the top layer on top of the bundt.

5. Pour the chocolate glaze over the bundt. Let it rest for at least 30 minutes to allow the glaze to set before serving.

(29) Snow Peaks Bundt

This bundt will satisfy even the choosiest gourmands. The raspberry and white chocolate combination makes for a simple preparation and simple appearance. Goes well with white wine or coffee.

Makes: 10

Preparation Time: 15 minutes

Total Cook Time: 25 minutes

List of Ingredients:

- Raspberries, 5 ⅓ oz.

- White baking chocolate, 7 oz.
- Eggs, 2
- Sunflower or rapeseed oil, 4 Tablespoons
- Confectioners sugar, 3 ½ oz.
- Salt, pinch
- Half & half, ⅖ cup
- Plain flour, 4 ⅕ oz.
- Cornstarch, 1 oz.
- Baking powder, 1 ½ teaspoons

MMMMMMMMMMMMMMMMMMMMMMMMMMMMMMM

Methods:

1. In a mixing bowl, combine the eggs and oil.

2. Add the salt, half & half, confectioners sugar, and vanilla sugar. Stir well to combine.

3. Add the flour, cornstarch, and baking powder. Stir well.

4. With a knife, chop a quarter of chocolate and add it to the mixing bowl.

5. Set aside 10 raspberries. Place the rest in the mixing bowl. Stir everything to combine.

6. Pour the mixture into a greased twelve cavity mini bundt pan. Bake for 25 minutes in a preheated oven at 350 °F.

7. Melt the rest of white chocolate over low heat. Use this as the frosting for the bundts. Place a raspberry in the dimple of each.

(30)   Granny's Chocolate Bundt

This recipe comes straight from my Granny's kitchen. It is truly an extraordinary bundt mad with two kinds of chocolate. It's very simple to make and has a unique taste. You'll be able to have any kind of beverage with this bundt.

Makes: 16

Preparation Time: 15-20 minutes

Total Cook Time: 1 hour

List of Ingredients:

- Dark baking chocolate, 3 ⅕ oz. for batter and 3 ½ oz. for glaze
- White baking chocolate, 3 ½ oz.
- Butter, 9 oz. for batter, 1 oz. for glaze, 1 oz. for greasing

- Sugar, 7 oz.
- Eggs, 5
- Plain flour, 13 oz.
- Baking powder, 1 packet
- Milk, ⅖ cup
- Breadcrumbs, ½ cup

MMMMMMMMMMMMMMMMMMMMMMMMMMMMMMMMMM

Methods:

1. Chop the dark and white chocolate (three and a half ounces of each) into small pieces.

2. In a mixing bowl, mix the butter and sugar and beat with a hand mixer until pale and foamy.

3. While continuing to mix, add the eggs one at the time.

4. Add the chopped chocolates, plain flour, baking powder, and milk. Stir everything well.

5. Grease a bundt pan with butter, then coat it with breadcrumbs. Shake out the excess.

6. Pour the batter in the bundt pan and bake in a preheated oven at 340 °F for one hour.

7. When the bundt is baked, melt the chocolate and butter over low heat. Pour the mixture over the bundt.

(31) Glazed Bundt Cake

This is the bundt I typically make for the Easter. A single batch is never enough, so I make three. It disappears extremely quickly. Serve with white wine, coffee, or milk. This cake is colorful and cheerful just like the Easter.

Makes: 16

Preparation Time: 25 minutes

Total Cook Time: 50 minutes

List of Ingredients:

- Mandarin oranges, 6
- Plain flour 6 ⅓ oz.
- Ground almonds, 10 ½ oz.

- Eggs, 4
- Butter, 6 ½ oz.
- Caster sugar, 7 oz., divided in halves
- Dry yeast, ½ Tablespoons
- Half & half, 1 cup
- Confectioners sugar, 7 oz.
- Egg white, 1
- Candied fruits mix, 4 oz.
- Salt, pinch

MMMMMMMMMMMMMMMMMMMMMMMMMMMMMMMMM

Methods:

1. Peel the mandarin oranges and squeeze their juice out and set aside. Grate the zest from the peel of two mandarin oranges and set aside.

2. In a mixing bowl, place the butter and half of caster sugar. Mix with a hand mixer until foamy.

3. While mixing, add one egg at the time until all are used.

4. Add the salt, flour, dry yeast, half & half, almonds, and mandarin orange zest. Stir well to combine.

5. Pour the mixture into a greased bundt pan. Bake in preheated oven at 350 °F for 50 minutes.

6. While the bundt is baking, place the mandarin oranges juice and other half of the caster sugar in a pan. Cook over medium-high heat until it thickens, 7-10 minutes.

7. When the bundt is cooked, let it rest for 5 minutes on a serving platter. Then, pour over it sugar syrup.

8. In a mixing bowl, mix the confectioners sugar and an egg white. Whisk the mixture well and use it for frosting the bundt. Garnish the bundt with the candied fruit mixture.

(32) Vermouth Bundt

The vermouth is a secret ingredient which gives this bundt a delicious aroma. Serve a dessert with it or some other digestif.

Makes: 16

Preparation Time: 25 minutes

Total Cook Time: 1 hour

List of Ingredients:

- Sugar, 10 ½ oz.
- Butter, 9 oz. and 1 oz. for greasing

- Eggs, 4
- Dried figs or raisins, 3 ½ oz.
- Vermouth, ⅘ cup
- Plain flour, 10 ½ oz.
- Baking powder, 1 packet
- Cornstarch, 1 tablespoon
- Cinnamon, 1 teaspoon
- Graham cracker crumbs, ¼ cup

MMMMMMMMMMMMMMMMMMMMMMMMMMMMMMMMM

Methods:

1. In a mixing bowl, combine the sugar and butter. Mix with a hand mixer until pale in color, velvety in texture, and all of the sugar has dissolved.

2. While continuing to mix, add the eggs one at a time until all eggs are used and the mixture is well combined.

3. Add the chopped figs or raisins, roughly chopped pieces of chocolate (roughly the size of the figs or raisins), and vermouth. Mix the ingredients well.

4. Sift the flour, baking powder, cornstarch, and cinnamon. Add this to the previous mixture and stir well to combine.

5. Grease a bundt pan with butter and coat with graham cracker crumbs. Shake out any excess.

6. Pour in the batter and bake in a preheated oven at 350 °F for one hour.

(33) Mini Bundt Cakes with Cream

A friend of mine told me that she loves this bundt recipe because it's baked in a pan with small cavities. She finds baking with a full-size bundt pan a bit daunting. Here you will not have such problems. Serve on plates with flower decorations and enjoy look and taste. This yellow bundt cake is best served with white wine, coffee, or milk.

Makes: 16

Preparation Time: 10 minutes

Total Cook Time: 20 minutes

List of Ingredients:

For batter:

- Plain flour, 1 ½ cup
- Sugar, 1 ⅘ cup
- Butter, 1 cup, cubed
- Vanilla, stick
- Eggs, 4
- Baking powder, 1 teaspoon

For cream:

- Butter, ⅔ cup
- Confectioners sugar, 10 ½ oz.
- Half & half, ⅕ cup
- Raspberry syrup, 1 tablespoon
- Red food color, few drops

MMMMMMMMMMMMMMMMMMMMMMMMMMMMMMMM

Methods:

For batter:

1. Scrape the seeds out of the vanilla pod and place it in a mixing bowl.

2. Add the cubes of butter, flour, baking powder, sugar, and eggs to the mixing bowl. Mix well until it becomes smooth.

3. Load the batter into a piping bag and fill the greased twelve cavity mini bundt pan. Bake for 20 minutes in a preheated oven at 350 °F. Each cavity fills up to ¾ inch from the lip.

For cream:

1. While the bundt cakes are baking, mix the butter and confectioners sugar in a mixing bowl. Mix with a hand mixer until foamy.

2. Add the half & half, raspberry syrup, and food color. Mix the ingredients until stiff.

When the bundt cakes are baked, leave them to cool. Use a piping bag to pipe the cream on them.

(34)   Colorful Bundt

This is such a colorful cake! Do not frost with icing sugar. You'll want the colors of the candied fruits to pop out. Serve with milk, coffee, or tea in morning. In the afternoon or evening, serve with white wine.

Makes: 16

Preparation Time: 15 minutes

Total Cook Time: 45 minutes

List of Ingredients:

- Butter, 2 sticks
- Confectioners sugar, 9 oz.
- Lemon zest, of half a lemon

- Eggs, 8, whites and yolks separated
- Candied fruits mix, 4 oz.
- Plain flour, 7 oz.

Methods:

1. In a mixing bowl butter, combine the sugar and lemon zest. Mix with a hand mixer until the mixture is foamy.

2. Add the egg yolks one at the time while continuing to mix with a hand mixer.

3. Add the candied fruits and stir well.

4. In another mixing bowl, beat the egg whites until they form stiff peaks. Then transfer them to a mixing bowl with the yolk and butter mixture. Stir gently to combine.

5. Add the plain flour and stir gently to combine.

6. Pour in the mixture to a greased bundt pan and bake in a preheated oven at 275 °F for 45 minutes.

(35) Chocolate Bundt

The name says it all. There's chocolate inside and chocolate outside. This cake is best served with red wine. For kids, it is a hearty breakfast, but it can also be breakfast for you, too.

Makes: 16

Preparation Time: 20 minutes

Total Cook Time: 40 minutes

List of Ingredients:

- Eggs, 6, separated yolks and whites
- Confectioners sugar, 5 oz.
- Baking chocolate, 2 oz. and 4 $1/5$ oz., melted

- Ground almonds, 5 oz.
- Sugar, 1 cup
- Water, ½ cup

MMMMMMMMMMMMMMMMMMMMMMMMMMMMMMMMMM

Methods:

1. In a mixing bowl, combine the confectioners sugar and egg yolks. Use a hand mixer to mix until foamy.

2. Add two ounces of melted chocolate, then mix well.

3. In another mixing bowl, beat the egg whites until they form stiff peaks.

4. Add the almonds and egg whites to the egg yolk mixture. Stir gently to combine.

5. Pour the mixture into a greased bundt pan and bake in a preheated oven at 400 °F for 40 minutes.

6. When the bundt cake is done, transfer it to a serving platter and let it cool.

7. While it's cooling, combine flour, a half ounce of chocolate, water, and sugar in a saucepan. Stir over low heat until the sugar melts.

8. Pour this chocolate glaze over the bundt.